NNSA Frontline Managers' Leadership Guide

TWELVE TRICKS TO MAKE LEADERSHIP, AND YOUR JOB, EASIER

Mike Mears

NNSA Frontline Managers' Leadership Guide

By Mike Mears

Copyright 2020 by Mike Mears

Kindle Edition

Copyright 2020 by Mike Mears
Researched and written by Mike Mears

All rights reserved. Without limiting the rights under the copyright reserved above, no part of this publication may be reproduced, stored in, or introduced into a retrieval system, or transmitted in any form or by any means (electronic, mechanical, photocopying, recording, or otherwise) without prior written permission.

For permission requests, please contact the author.

Published in USA.

Table of Contents

Table of Contents

Introduction for NNSA Frontline Managers

CHAPTER 1: What Makes Employees Tick?

    Our Survival Instinct and the Savannah River Paradox

    Social Survival Instinct: What do Employees Really Want to Know?

CHAPTER 2: Be a Great NNSA Leader—Key Behaviors

    Three Big Leadership Behaviors

CHAPTER 3: Take a Short Cut, Copy Your Best Boss

    Why are Behaviors so Important?

    BEHAVIORAL TEMPLATE

CHAPTER 4: How to Define Your Leadership Philosophy

    LEADERSHIP BEHAVIOR ASSESSMENT

CHAPTER 5: How to Create a Leadership Habit

    TIPS TO CHANGE HABITS

CHAPTER 6: How to Not (Inadvertently) Be a Bad Boss

    A Little Brain Science

CHAPTER 7: How to Use Emotional Intelligence (or EQ)

    Five Elements of Emotional Intelligence (Daniel Goleman)

    Three Steps to Use EQ

CHAPTER 8: How to Motivate Others

    Examples of Motivational Awards

    Ideas to Help Motivate NNSA Employees

    NNSA Employees' Golden Offer to Managers

CHAPTER 9: How to Use Insight Prompts

- What is Insight?
- Why is This Important to Frontline Managers?
- Examples of Insight Prompts
- How You Can Conduct a Leadership Review
- Keys to a Productive Leadership Review Session
- In Closing

CHAPTER 10: How to Easily Give and Receive Feedback

- Check-Ins
- Positive Feedback
- Brain Trick 1: Always Use Future Tense
- Brain Trick 2: Ask For Feedback
- Brain Trick 3: Ask For Permission to Give or Get Feedback
- Brain Trick 4: Ask For Feedback on Getting Feedback
- *Quotes*

CHAPTER 11: How to Listen Actively

- SIX SKILLS THAT CONTRIBUTE TO ACTIVE LISTENING

CHAPTER 12: How to Ask Powerful Questions

- *Quote*

CHAPTER 13: Leadership Tip Sheet

CHAPTER 14: Recommended Reading

- Background a
About The Author

Introduction for NNSA Frontline Managers

Are there days when nothing you do as a leader seems to work? Are you willing to take a short journey with this e-book to upend much of what you've learned about management to make your day easier?

A more natural way to manage appears if you take a little time to think about how employees' brains work and don't work. The mind is a miracle, but it doesn't operate the way we assume in traditional management theory. For instance, our brains are a bit outdated for the modern world, so using simple logic to lead them is not as powerful as we presume.

Because of the way the brain operates, you face three managerial constraints every day:

1. If you tell them, they won't listen.
2. What's in their heads is not in yours.
3. They won't tell you what's in their heads.

This guide offers you a series of useful techniques to break through organizational inertia and your employees' resistance to change.

The key to making your job easier is realizing that our brains are not the logical machines we think they are. Frontline managers who don't appreciate the power of what scientists call the automatic brain (System 1) are continuously surprised at how subordinates react and don't react. The automatic brain houses our instincts, drives, and emotions.

The reason for this is that humans use their logical brain (System 2) far less than their automatic brain. That's why you need to find the keys that unlock the automatic brain.

This guide offers 12 ways to get inside other people's heads (and your own!) to accomplish your vision and goals.

For instance, the chapter on *Insight Prompts* shows you how to nudge others to reflect and have aha! moments. Small epiphanies or insights can help them overcome their automatic brains' innate resistance to change. The *Insight Prompt* is one of the several powerful leadership tools in this book.

There are also chapters to help you trick your brain. The *Active Listening* chapter shows you ways to avoid jumping to conclusions. You learn more when you listen actively, and it helps build trust.

Keep this book close at hand. Every day, copy and practice a few of the behaviors listed in the chapter on *Great Leadership*. I have isolated these in a study of 200 top CIA, DOD, and NNSA leaders. Apply all 10 of these techniques to improve NNSA's culture and inspire your workforce.

Best wishes in building your leadership legacy,

Mike Mears

CHAPTER 1:
What Makes Employees Tick?

When dealing with people, it's helpful to consider the basic drives, aspirations, and even hidden fears lodged inside their heads. A quick overview of the brain and how it drives human nature will help you understand why people avoid change on one hand and take risk and achieve great things on the other.

When dealing with subordinates, we encounter three basic management constraints:

1) If you tell them, they won't listen

2) What's in their heads is not in yours

3) They won't tell you what's in their heads

All three constraints spring from the way our automatic brain works, so let's start with what psychologists know about the human brain. The following is what you already discovered in your Role of a Supervisor training:

- We are more irrational than we think we are.
- We are social animals and highly emotional.
- Our basic instinct is survival. This instinct is hidden in our brain, but it dictates most of our actions and reactions. It is a bit outdated for the modern workplace.
- We constantly look for small signals. In life and work, it's little things that count.
- We all resist change. (It's a survival mechanism.)
- Everything in our heads (motives, values, and experience) is invisible to others. They can only see our behaviors.
- In many cases, others will misperceive our behaviors.
- In many cases, insights (aha! moments) can help overcome change resistance.

Here is a simplified brain model:

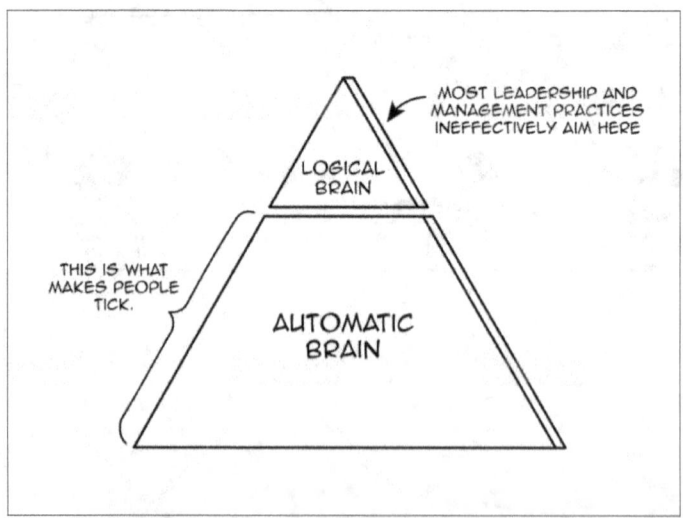

The central point is that you can't persuade or implement change with logic alone. Have you ever won a political argument using facts? Leading people at work with just logic doesn't work too well either. An even simpler way to think about this is that the top of the triangle represents your head and the bottom is your heart and gut. You can spend all day attempting to convince your employee's head about something, but if their heart and gut don't agree, you won't get anywhere.

Psychologists think of this in another way. They separate the brain into two parts:
- The System 1 brain is fast, automatic, and intuitive.
- The System 2 brain, or logical brain, is analytical and logical.

We will focus on the automatic brain, because it contains what makes people tick: motivations, values, biases, and assumptions. It holds our human nature, and it is the human nature with its innate change resistance that defeats most management practices.

You'll save lots of time, frustration, and energy by thinking about how others think and feel. Why? Because all of us spend most of our time outside our logical brain.

The chapters in this guide offer ideas to help you influence the automatic brain so that you can more easily lead, influence, and motivate your team.

Our Survival Instinct and the Savannah River Paradox

We still carry around our ancestors' instinct to survive. But survival does not just mean physical survival; social survival is important too. We are social animals, and we pay attention to a vast number of cues coming from others, including behaviors as simple as a smile or a wave. How well our peers respect us or what a person in authority thinks of us is crucial to us.

During a Quick Win exercise at the Department of Energy's nuclear and environmental facility at the Savannah River Site (SRS), a group of employees complained about the lack of communication in the organization. Approximately 40% of the issues brought up during these Quick Win sessions at other public and private sector organizations center on communication shortfalls as well, so the complaint is typical.

> ### How to do a "Quick Win"
>
> *With the boss out of the room, employees brainstorm ideas that can help them do their jobs better or make their office lives a little easier—and ultimately more pleasurable.*
>
> *Once they generate some ideas for improvement, they can call the supervisor in for a briefing. It's the supervisor's job to decide whether to approve the idea on the spot and then provide top cover so that the employees can begin implementation.*
>
> *The ideas are generally little things, but remember, little things are important.*

Later, in the same Quick Win exercise, the employees complained about having too many staff meetings. I was confused. How could there be insufficient communication yet too many meetings? The answer was that what employees craved was personal feedback that couldn't be provided in a meeting. Organizational meetings don't and can't scratch the itch of what employees really want to know.

Social Survival Instinct: What Do Employees Want to Know?

- What's going on in the back of the boss's mind? Is he/she happy with me?

- What does the boss expect of me? What are my unstated responsibilities?
- What do my peers think of me?
- What's the big picture? Where are we going?
- How is my job linked to the big picture?
- How am I performing? Will I be evaluated in a fair manner?
- Can I experiment on the job? Where are the "get-in-trouble" fences? Where does the boss want me between free-wheeling and by-the-book?
- What is the leadership philosophy of my new boss? Will he/she be dictatorial? Will his/her bosses allow abusive behaviors?
- How well am I fitting in around here?
- Is company leadership considering reorganizing? How will that affect me?
- What else is being planned that might affect me?
- Am I making a difference? How can I contribute and add value here?

Note: Have you answered all these questions today for your employees? Of course not—it would take half your day. You will find that once you apply the tips in this e-book, most of the employee concerns and fears listed above will magically melt away.

CHAPTER 2:
Be a Great NNSA Leader—Key Behaviors

When I was chief of human capital at CIA, employees provided me with 8,000 ratings of their bosses on a five-point scale. They classified 17% of bosses in the top category, *great*, and provided a list of descriptors, such as accessible, trustworthy, and self-aware. Paradoxically, the list was not helpful in teaching frontline managers because psychologists tell us everyone thinks they have integrity, good character, and so forth—this blind spot on ourselves is one of many cognitive biases. It is called the *Lake Woebegone effect* or the *Better-than-average effect*.

A separate study I completed of 200 Great-rated Agency (and later NNSA) bosses drilled in on simple behaviors rather than attributes. It uncovered simple behaviors that could be categorized into three groups: valuing others, giving, and providing deep communication. Managers practicing a significant number of these behaviors build psychological safety, trust, clarity, and motivation within their workforces. (If you are familiar with emotional intelligence, or EQ, note the similarity in the high-impact practices. EQ is briefly covered in the next chapter.)

- **Establish safety:** Value others and show concern
- **Build trust:** Give (law of reciprocity), i.e., make more deposits than withdrawals
- **Create clarity:** Connect with deeper two-way communications

Three Big Leadership Behaviors

	Behavior	Examples	What it does	Your to-do list
Establish Safety	Value others	Smile, say hello, be positive, show appreciation, use levity, play to their strengths, identify interests and needs, show concern, use appropriate empathy, and listen	Overcomes subconscious fears, removes perception of hostility, projects an appropriate level of friendliness, signals humanness, and shows that you value others as individuals	1) 2) 3)
Build Trust	Give (law of reciprocity)	Share knowledge/expertise, vision, time, recognition, opportunity, respect, and power, listen, and invite participation: ask for employee opinions and ideas and act on them; where possible, involve them in decision-making	Builds trust, establishes fairness, signals respect, empowers, motivates, and prompts better upward feedback (also good for influencing others outside the management chain)	1) 2) 3)
Create Clarity	Connect (deep communication)	Tell stories, make symbolic actions, have one-on-one conversations, ask what if, how, and why questions, and listen	Provides clarity of vision, mission, and guidelines. Defines appropriate risk levels. Allows a meeting of the minds.	1) 2) 3)

The fourth category of behaviors, the *insight prompt*, involves challenging others to think and reflect. It has proven to be a powerful management tool because it overcomes change resistance in others. It is covered more in detail under the heading "How to use insight prompts."

Launch Change				
	Only Then... Challenge with insight prompts	Give homework, e.g., "give me three ideas on this in one week." Ask power questions. Jointly agree on objectives	Provides a heads-up, challenges without creating emotional pain, and positively prompts action	1) 2) 3)

Quote

"Talk to people. Get out and walk and repeat the message as often as possible. Communicate in writing, communicate on the phone, and communicate online. But more important than any of that is the art of listening and finding ways by which your team can communicate with you. That's a more subtle and difficult task, but without it, you are actually hampering yourself...they'll only tell you the truth if they trust that they won't be harmed by it."

– Bruce Hart, retired government executive

CHAPTER 3:
Take a Short Cut, Copy Your Best Boss

Changing behavior to self-improve can be as difficult as dieting. We've all practiced habit-breaking routines. We start with enthusiasm. Then we falter "just once." Soon, it's "maybe another." And before we know it, we give up.

Fortunately, by boosting our awareness and copying a few behaviors practiced by great leaders, we can achieve significant personal improvements.

Focus on your best boss's behaviors and not his or her stated values.

Many believe integrity is the foundation of great leadership. Although that may be true, there is a catch: all of us believe we have integrity. It's one of those little human quirks.

Start by asking the crucial question: "What's inside our heads?" If you list your answer, be sure to include ideas, biases, opinions, hopes, memories, goals, values, fears, and beliefs.

This exercise produced interesting insights. The first is that each of these items are universal; all humans store all of these in their brains. However, what is inside each category of ideas, opinions, etc., is completely different for each individual, showing that everyone's reality is just a little bit different. The biggest insight is that all of these ideas are buried in someone's head, meaning they are almost invisible to the rest of us.

Why Are Behaviors So Important?

In terms of human relationships, the final insight is the most critical. The values housed inside our heads are quite visible to us but are completely invisible to others. Outsiders are left to observe our behaviors and deduce our values from them. So, when it comes to other people's perceptions of us, our behaviors are crucial. Remember that old axiom, "Actions speak louder than words."

Recall the leadership study in which I collected employee ratings and descriptors on 8,000 bosses. Employees described their best bosses as honest, sharing, positive, and trustworthy, along with other constructive attributes such as "has integrity."

The descriptors were accurate but fuzzy. If others can't see my positivity or my integrity like I do, how should I behave to show these attributes to them? The answer came through storytelling.

Over 200 employees told me stories about their best bosses. In each case, they described a boss's behavior that positively affected them, and I organized the behaviors into four categories.

Interestingly, the behaviors mirrored 1) current leadership best practices, 2) emotional intelligence theory, and 3) the way our grandmothers told us to act. The categories sound like clichés until we look at the specific behaviors described within.

These leadership behaviors can be applied in everyday life, practiced daily, and provide a roadmap to better ourselves. Here is another way to think about them: value others, give, involve, and connect. As you read them below, recall what you liked about your boss's behaviors.

Value Others

This involves acknowledging people. Carol, one of the 200 employees, told me about her previous boss, Lester, who strode past employees every morning with his brow furrowed and head down.

Carol was an experienced coach and a gifted feedback giver. She broke this news to Lester:

Carol: "They think you're mad at them."

Lester: "Who?"

Carol: "The employees. They think you are mad because you don't say 'hello,' and you don't smile."

Lester (after some stammering): "You know I do that. I'm actually a bit of an introvert."

Carol: "But your employees misinterpret that as disinterest or even anger."

Lester began smiling more often and pushed himself to say "Good morning." After that, his unit scored well in employee surveys. There were numerous reasons for the higher rankings, but I like to think that Lester's behavioral change helped.

This group of behaviors builds psychological or social safety inside your organization.

Give & Involve

This uses the law of reciprocity found in psychology and anthropology. For instance, share your expertise and knowledge with others to build trust. It's not the gift that builds trust but the consistency of giving and helping others.

I observed one fast food manager, Rene, as he regularly rolled up his sleeves to help his crew. Every day, he gave helpful advice and recognition. His employees reciprocated with loyalty, hard work, and respect.

I asked him about the secret to good leadership. He answered, "I like to make more deposits than withdrawals." It was a concise behavioral guide for building trust. When you involve others, they feel you are giving them a little piece of the pie. The best boss stories underscored the fact that when appropriate, great leaders will invite employees into decision-making and planning. Having a piece of the pie motivates us because it gives us a sense of control over our work. This same sharing principle applies to daily life.

Whenever possible, include others. Invite participation.

Connect

Meetings and e-mails often swamp this principle because it requires personal two-way communications.

Don't engage in high-level platitudes (use dialogue).

And remember, face-to-face always beats e-mail! Employees described their best bosses as great listeners. None of the four behaviors takes as long to do—connecting can be as quick as a hallway conversation.

I CAN'T GO YET. I STILL NEED TO E-MAIL TOM HE'S GETTING PLUCKED AND BASTED WEDNESDAY.

The behaviors overlap. An "Attaboy" or "Attagirl" is a connection, but it is also a gift.

Acknowledging others as we step into the office is both an example of a connection and a signal that we value them. Whenever you are in doubt about any of the behaviors, just ask, "What would my best boss do?"

Becoming a better leader or person really is this simple, but consistently following these behaviors is devilishly difficult—remember the dieting example? The behaviors may be simple but difficult to practice because of our varying degrees of self-awareness, distraction, and the gravitational pull of habit.

Practice your best boss's behaviors. Now think back to your best boss. Use the *Behavioral Template* on the next page to jog your memory and list the things they did that you admired. (If you want a hard copy of the template, go to **https://www.mikemears.com**)

BEHAVIORAL TEMPLATE

Behavior: Value Others

Examples: *Smile, say hello, be positive, show appreciation, use levity, identify interests and needs, show concern, and use appropriate empathy*

What it does: *Overcomes subconscious fears, removes perception of hostility, projects an appropriate level of friendliness, and shows that you value others as individuals*

What your best boss did:
_____
_____
_____

Behavior: Give (Law of Reciprocity)

Examples: *Share knowledge/expertise, vision, time, recognition, opportunity, respect, and power*

What it does: *Builds trust, good for influencing others outside the management chain, and establishes fairness*

What your best boss did:
_____
_____
_____

Behavior: Invite Participation

Examples: *Ask for employee opinions and ideas and act on them; where possible, involve others in decision-making*

What it does: *Signals respect, empowers, motivates, and prompts better upward feedback*

What your best boss did:

_____
_____
_____

Behavior: Connect (Deep Communication)

Examples: *Listen, tell stories, one-on-one conversations, and ask what if, how, and why questions*

What it does: *Provides clarity, defines appropriate risk levels, and allows the meeting of the minds*

What your best boss did:

_____
_____
_____

Your list is complete. What's the next step?

Have you ever noticed that everything on your to-do list involves administration and busy work? There is nothing spelled out on your list to improve relationships. To the automatic brain, little things mean a lot.

One way to bypass the gravity of distraction and habit is to transfer few of the simple behaviors you listed in the template to you daily to-do list. It's just like recording what you eat in a diet diary to develop better eating habits. Be specific: "Say hello to Jessica."

Adopting the behaviors and then crossing them off the list gives you a refreshing jolt of dopamine, the brain chemical controlling pleasure and pain. But there is much more. Practice a few behaviors every day to build safety and trust with others, and you've made your workplace, and the world, a better place.

CHAPTER 4:
How to Define Your Leadership Philosophy

Your leadership philosophy is not an aspirational list like the New Year's resolutions: "I will be a role model; I will live my values; I will do better." Your real philosophy is the way you presently behave. Your philosophy is expressed through your actions. Your employees perceive (or misperceive) your behaviors to determine in their mind how good of a leader you really are.

The first rule of leadership is "know thyself;" it means you have to go through a mildly painful self-analysis to determine which of your behaviors you need to change.

If you are like most of us, you assume you are doing pretty well. You may think your behaviors are understood by others. But remember what we observed in the "What makes employees tick" section:

- We are all more irrational than we think we are.
- The values, aspirations, and beliefs we carry around in your head are invisible to others.
- Other people can only see our behaviors, and— given the chance— they will misinterpret them. (In psychology, this is called *negativity bias*.)

Designing and enacting your leadership philosophy is a never-ending process. No one displays all the great-leader behaviors listed under the "How to be a great leader" section. Your current behaviors become habitual, and, from what we know about the difficulty of changing a habit, no one can suddenly change and implement all of them at once.

The trick is to start with one behavior, master it, and then move on to the next. It may be best to start with changing a behavior that is the most distasteful to others or with adopting the one that will have the greatest positive impact on others.

Now fill out the *Leadership Behavior Assessment* on the next page. (If you want a hard copy of the assessment, go to https://www.mikemears.com)

LEADERSHIP BEHAVIOR ASSESSMENT

Answer the questions in this three-step process:

1. Current Status

a. How do you think others perceive you?

_____

b. How did you get this feedback? (Directly from others, assessments, other.)

_____

c. How would you like to be perceived?

_____

d. How would that benefit you and others?

_____

2. New Habit

a. What will be your initial leadership philosophy? (No more than three sentences.)

b. What specific behaviors will you change/add to live your leadership philosophy? (Feel free to copy some from your best boss.)

_____

c. How will you create and reinforce a new habit?

_____

3. Follow-up

a. Has your new behavior become a habit?

_____

b. What has worked or not worked and why?

_____

c. Have you tweaked the behavior? How?

_____

d. How will you get feedback about the results?

_____

e. What do you need to change next?

_____

Let's be honest about this: it isn't easy. Modifying your behavior to become a great leader is as difficult as quitting smoking. So, use the tips in the next chapter on how to change a habit.

CHAPTER 5:
How to Create a Leadership Habit

What is a Habit?

It is a settled or regular tendency or practice that is especially hard to give up.

What are examples of good leadership habits to copy?

- Smile, say hello, and be positive.
- Show appreciation and use levity.
- Identify employee interests and needs.
- Show concern.
- Share knowledge/expertise, vision, time, recognition, and opportunity.
- Ask for employee opinions and ideas and act on them.
- When possible, involve others in decision-making.
- Have one-on-one conversations.
- Ask *what if*, *how*, and *why* questions and use insight pushes.

How do habits form?

A habit starts with a psychological pattern called a "habit loop," which is a three-part process:

1. First is a cue, or trigger, that tells your brain to go into automatic mode and let a behavior unfold.
2. Next is the routine, which is the behavior itself. This is what we imagine when we think about habits.
3. Last is a reward. Positive brain chemicals are released, and the brain remembers the habit loop in the future.

Once a behavior becomes automatic, it is stored in the automatic brain, and the logical part of your brain goes into a type of sleep mode.

TIPS TO CHANGE HABITS

- Start with one habit.
- Write it down and visualize success.
- Think about what you will do and not what you will stop doing.
- Take small steps.
- Motivation comes in waves; seize it.
- Practice new behaviors in the morning.
- Use a visual cue to reinforce it: a visible calendar, a post-it note, etc.

Steps to changing a habit

1. Solicit feedback from a colleague on something they perceive about you that you would like to change.

2. Reflect on how you might implement some of the tips above and set a timeline to begin changing the habit.
3. Each week, briefly reflect on how you feel you are doing with regard to your habit change.
4. Follow-up with your colleague/spouse in a set timeframe (weeks/months) and see if/how their perception has changed.
5. Repeat.

▶ **Remember, an old habit, like sticking close to your office, keeps you from improving as a leader. Once you've practiced a new habit for a while, say chatting with employees in the cafeteria, it becomes ingrained and becomes a natural part of you. A new habit makes you a better leader.**

CHAPTER 6:
How To Not (Inadvertently) Be a Bad Boss

The descriptors I gathered from CIA employees on bad bosses exemplified behaviors that shut down employee creativity and thinking. Many of them describe autocratic or micromanaging behaviors.

In a nutshell, bad bosses inflict something UCLA neuroscientist Matthew Lieberman calls social pain. Per Lieberman's experiments, our prefrontal cortex shuts down when we sense the following:

1. Things are out of control.
2. Our status is challenged.
3. Something seems unfair.

Here is a partial listing of dreadful bosses' behaviors that make employees feel like things are out of their control, a personal insult, or unfair. When we experience perceived abuse from anyone, including our boss, we register emotional pain in our brains, which degrades our mental performance.

Bad boss descriptors to avoid:

> Abusive, screamer, rules-driven, disengaged, inconsistent, unwilling to listen, indecisive, intolerant, divisive, narrow, rigid, loner, unfair, condescending, self-serving, incompetent, paranoid, untrusting, self-absorbed, disloyal, dishonest, uncommunicative, back-stabbing, non-supportive, and closed-minded.

Note: Frontline managers need to understand the social pain concept. We all have emotional hair triggers, and we respond to any perceived bad behavior from our boss. If employees feel you have tripped one of the bad boss descriptors above, and if their perception is left unaddressed, it will lead to future supervisory problems and reduced organizational performance.

How do you know how employees perceive you? Getting feedback is crucial. We cover this under "How to easily give and receive feedback" and "How to listen actively."

A Little Brain Science

Social pain is a result of interpersonal rejection, unfairness, and uncertainty, and it significantly reduces cognitive ability.

Recent studies show the following:

- People differ in their degrees of sensitivity to social pain.
- Social pain and physical pain follow the same circuitry and "light up" the same brain regions.
- Memories of social pain often last longer and with higher intensity than memories of physical pain.

Merely thinking about a past episode of social pain reduces one's ability to perform mental tests.

There is an exception to the *if you tell them, they won't listen* rule. Employees don't hear what you say unless it is an uncaring comment, as shown in the cartoon.

The offending remark could be off the cuff or even intended in jest. But employees can and will misinterpret, hence the importance of receiving ongoing feedback.

Threats to any of the following five items create social pain (strong negative emotions):

- Status
- Certainty
- Autonomy
- Relatedness
- Fairness

Status depicts our relative importance to others. A perception of lowered status reduces cognitive ability.

> Weak leaders do not provide sufficient positive feedback, and their relationships lack two-way involvement with employees.

> Good leaders make people feel better about themselves. They invite participation and don't dictate.

>> Questions for you: *How can you preserve people's status and sense of self-worth during change? Can you provide more positive feedback?*

Certainty is our ability to predict the future. For your mind, negative certainty is better than uncertainty; that is why people resist you changing a dissatisfactory status quo.

> Weak leaders fail to communicate, or they transmit unclear or ambiguous expectations.

> Good leaders set, share, and reinforce clear expectations.

>> Questions for you: *How can you provide some degree of certainty during change? Can you share your thoughts with employees?*

Autonomy represents our sense of control over events. For all of us, even having a small choice is beneficial. Micromanaging elicits a strong threat response.

Autocratic leaders make top-down decisions. They micromanage with no input.

Good leaders allow involvement in decision-making.

> *Questions for you: How can you offer people control over aspects of change? In what areas can you give them more autonomy? Can you more broadly engage your employees in change planning/doing?*

Relatedness describes our sense of safety with others. Lack of safe social interactions generates a threat response. Often, small groups and personal interactions promote trust.

Aloof leaders maintain what they think is a professional distance. They engage in task-focused interactions only.

Good leaders foster personal relations and trust. They build connections and teams.

> *Questions for you: How can you embrace connections and feelings of inclusion during change? Can you create shared goals among people and groups?*

Fairness characterizes our sense of fair exchanges between people. Fair exchanges are intrinsically rewarding. Unfairness at work affects mental and physical health.

Unfair leaders make decisions that seem inequitable. They fail to make processes transparent.

Good leaders demonstrate fairness in interactions and decision-making.

> Questions for you: *How will you demonstrate fairness and transparency in the change process? Can you involve others in decision-making to some degree?*

Whenever one of the five big social pain originators listed above is triggered, a flood of chemicals washes over the brain, causing emotional distress in the form of sadness, anger, depression, or various other negative emotions. When this happens, fMRI (functional magnetic resonance imaging) displays show energy draining out of the logical prefrontal cortex accompanied by a flare-up of the emotional limbic system.

We may fool ourselves that we are autonomous human beings. In actuality, we are all very much social beings concerned about status, unfairness, and loss of control: in short, our sense of social safety within a group matters to us. The modern-day office is a soup of social pain, so your first job as a frontline manager is to do no harm and ensure that you are not inflicting social pain.

Social pain has a long-lasting effect on individuals, and it is very real to them. As frontline managers, we are in a position to inadvertently inflict social pain on others. We, as leaders, need to keep this in mind.

Quotes

"I think the thing that put me off the most was witnessing somebody in a leadership position in a dictatorial mode, ranting and raving. People don't leave jobs, they leave supervisors."
– Pat Hanback, retired government executive

"I worked for a particularly awful person who was in a very senior position. That person was a screamer and routinely demeaned people in front of other people. It was really a nightmare and the only thing that got me through it was protecting the people under me. People who don't give you good direction and guidance, and then turn around and belittle you for not giving them what they want, are not leaders."

– Mary Corrado, retired government executive

CHAPTER 7:
How to Use Emotional Intelligence (or EQ)

Emotional intelligence refers to the ability to identify and manage one's own emotions and the emotions of others. According to psychologists, it includes at least three skills: emotional awareness, or the ability to identify and name one's own emotions; the ability to harness those emotions and apply them to tasks such as thinking and problem-solving; and the ability to manage emotions, which includes both regulating one's own feelings when necessary and understanding and interacting well with the emotions of others .

Five Elements of Emotional Intelligence (Daniel Goleman)

1. **Empathy:** This is the ability to understand or feel what another person is experiencing from within their frame of reference, i.e., the ability to place oneself in another's position.

    a. Pay attention to body language.

    b. Respond to feelings.

2. **Self-Awareness:** This is the art of understanding yourself, recognizing what stimuli you're facing, and then preparing for how to manage yourself in a proactive and reactive manner.

    a. Leaders who focus on building both internal and external self-awareness, who seek honest feedback from critics, and who ask *what* instead of *why* can learn to see themselves more clearly—and reap the many rewards that increased self-knowledge delivers.

    b. Keep a journal to increase self-awareness, and learn to slow down and examine *why* before reacting.

3. **Self-Regulation:** Leaders who effectively regulate themselves rarely verbally attack others, make rushed or emotional decisions, stereotype people, or compromise their values. Self-regulation is all about staying in control.

    a. Know your values and practice being calm.

    b. Using your self-awareness skills can help you understand the stimuli that sets you off and allows you to preemptively regulate emotions that you know are coming.

4. **Social Skills:** Leaders who do well in the social skills element of emotional intelligence are great communicators. They're just as open to hearing bad news as they are to hearing good news, and they're expert at getting their team to support them and be excited about a new mission or project.

    a. Learn conflict resolution.

    b. Learn how to praise others.

5. **Motivation:** Self-motivated leaders consistently work toward their goals and have extremely high standards for the quality of their work.

    a. Re-examine why you're doing your job, be hopeful, and find something good.

**To be effective, leaders must have a solid understanding of how their emotions and actions affect others. The better a leader relates to and works with others, the more successful he/she will be.

Three Steps to Use EQ

Emotional Intelligence isn't just useless, yet interesting, knowledge. Applying Emotional Intelligence to your daily interactions in the workplace will help you build better relationships with your staff and co-workers and will also allow you to be a better manager.

1. Have emotional awareness, or the ability to name your own emotions.

    See Chapter 10 on Feedback

2. Harness those emotions and practice applying them at work, home and in public.

    See Chapter 5 on Habit and Chapter 11 Active Listening

3. Manage your emotions.

    See Chapter 4 on Enacting Your Leadership Philosophy and Chapter 10 on Getting Feedback

CHAPTER 8:
How to Motivate Others

Motivation is what drives us daily as we go about our work. Having positive motivation can encourage workers to accomplish their (and your) goals and can drive up productivity. Having a lack of motivation, either personally or due to the working environment, can drain the individual and sink productivity. Whenever you, as a leader, have the chance to motivate those around, it's important that you take it. Doing so can drastically change your work environment.

Keys to Motivation
- Recognition
- Meaningful responsibility
- Camaraderie (peer relationships)
- Accomplishment

New Findings
- Fear narrows creativity
- Blue collar work—extrinsic or physical rewards work best
- White collar work—intrinsic or psychic rewards work best

Remember
- As a boss, you need to ponder on "what makes people tick."
- What motivates one person may not motivate another.
- Intrinsic rewards are more powerful than extrinsic rewards, so you don't need to rush to give

bonuses until you've dispensed lots of *attaboys* and *attagirls*.

Examples of Motivational Awards

Intrinsic (non-physical)	Extrinsic
Recognition and praise	Pay
Status	Bonus
Sense of achievement	Improved working conditions
Pride from the job	Promotion
Autonomy—work freedom	Fringe benefits
Learning	Time off

Ideas to Help Motivate NNSA Employees

- Practice the behaviors under the "How to be a great leader" section	- Find out what motivates them
- Start scheduling more one-on-one time	- Ask follow-up questions
- Provide resources so that employees can do their jobs well	- Praise and compliment them often
- Create purposeful work	- Help them develop new skills
- Actively involve them	- Believe in them

NNSA Employees' Golden Offer to Managers

"Don't keep us in the dark, clearly let us know what you want and why, be positive, give us leeway to be creative, tell us how we are doing, and we'll perform superbly for you."

CHAPTER 9:
How to Use Insight Prompts

What is Insight?

The sudden appearance of a solution through insight—the well-known *aha effect*—is a peculiar phenomenon that people have when they suddenly solve a problem. An insight can change one's view and help overcome natural resistance to change. A big one, called an epiphany, can change your life.

Insights occur when someone is relaxed, and that is not a condition easily experienced in today's hectic workplace with meetings and insight demands. How can you nudge employees to reflect and have insights to spur more creativity or help you implement change?

Why is This Important to Frontline Managers?

Implementing change calls for leadership—perhaps you want higher productivity or better performance or you have a change in mission. These involve a behavioral change in your employees, so you have to lead them to perform differently.

Your dilemma: We all resist changing behaviors, and your employees are just like the rest of us.

Your solution: Insights, or aha moments, release brain chemicals that help us overcome our natural resistance to change.

Science Daily notes, "The literature on insight lists four main characteristics of this experience:

- **Suddenness:** The occurrence is surprising and immediate.
- **Ease:** Compared with the obstacles experienced before, the task solution proceeds smoothly and efficiently.
- **Positive affect:** Insights yield positive affective experience.
- **The feeling of being right:** After an insight, problem-solvers judge the solution as being accurate and have confidence in this judgment, even before assessing its correctness."

Definition of an insight prompt

Think of an *insight prompt* as mental homework with a little accountability attached. Let's say your team is not as cohesive as you would like, and you want better group collaboration. Ask one of your employees,

"Sarah, I'd like to hear your ideas. Can you meet with me Tuesday with three or four ideas on how you think we can improve collaboration here?"

1. You gave Sarah mental homework.
2. Accountability is attached because Sarah knows she has to report back on Tuesday.

3. Sarah will have bought into her ideas and won't resist you implementing them. She will be pleased.

Sarah will be thinking about your problem until next Tuesday. You gave her a polite nudge that prompted her to reflect; this can lead to her having an insight or two. This can further lead to far less resistance to change on her part to the solution.

> **Insight prompt:** A leader's amicable question or command to generate a follower's insight. It provides time for reflection, a sense of autonomy, a realistic time constraint, and follow-up.

(To download a hard copy of the action plan on the next page, go to https://www.mikemears.com)

Your five-step insight prompt action plan

1. Define the outcome you want (e.g., more teamwork).

   _____

2. Define who the target is (e.g., your employee, Tom).

   _____

3. Craft a question or command to force them to think about the outcome (e.g., Tom, what can you do to foster teamwork?).

   _____

4. Set a time, deliver the prompt, and give them a set time to think about your question or command (Tom, what two things can you do to help improve teamwork? Let's meet Wednesday at 10:00 to discuss).

   Date, time, and location:
   _____

5. Follow up (hold your Wednesday meeting and have an informal chat).
   List Tom's ideas:
   _____

6. Define the outcome you want (ex. More teamwork).
   _____

Repeat this process to create organizational habit.

Examples of Insight Prompts

- **Classic prompt:** "Get back to me in a week with three ideas to improve your workplace." Or, "Wednesday, I'd like to hear your ideas on how we could improve our performance."

- **Rally your armies:** Armies include recent training graduates, new employees, other frontline managers, your peers, and affinity and training support groups. Can you enlist their support? For instance, ask one of them for support on a project to improve performance over the next six months.

- **Power questions:** Questions force the brain to stop, consider, and think; imperatives and statements don't. Don't put anyone on the spot—give them time to think and get back to you. *Why* and *how* are the most robust power questions. But *what* questions can be powerful as well:

    - What's possible here?
    - What stops us from taking more risks, and what can we do about it?
    - What assumptions hold us back, and can we change them?
    - What does it take to be successful in our organization?

  (Read more about this in "How to ask powerful questions.")

- **Employ prompt cascades:** Prompt reflection and thinking among several of your direct reports at once. For example, have your employees pick one improvement area from a recent climate survey to improve. Ask one employee to facilitate conversations among their peers on ways to improve. Or, ask a direct report to meet with his/her peers to come up with four suggestions for improvement. Listen to what they've come up with and then tell them to implement their suggestions.

- **Liberatingstructures.com:** This website offers 35 easy-to-use tools for quickly bringing a large number of people to an agreement. The tools help unleash creativity and gain buy-in, and they can generate mass insights. This site can be overwhelming, so simply focus on three of these methods or tools. Hint: 1-2-3-All is an excellent one for you to use, especially for getting people to accept change.

- **Conduct leadership reviews:** These are similar to budget reviews. They are a pre-scheduled interactive session with your employees to discuss pre-published questions concerning progress on motivation, culture change, new ideas, better collaboration, and integration. Reviews are upbeat and positive—no gotchas. They center on leadership and not on HR issues.

How You Can Conduct a Leadership Review

Give your employees the questions 30 days in advance so that they have time to meet, think, and act on them. Examples of leadership review questions include the following:

1. What have you collectively done to improve integration within our organization?

2. Describe three fresh ideas you or your peers had that you put into practice.

3. What shortcoming from our last employee climate survey will you focus on improving? How can we address it? How can we measure improvement?

4. How would you characterize our culture, and how do you think it contributes to employee performance? Any things we can do to make it even better.

5. What technique can I use to get better feedback?

6. What steps can we take to build trust?

7. Describe one leadership best practice you have seen elsewhere that we could adopt.

Keys to a Productive Leadership Review Session

- Questions distributed beforehand to prompt both thinking and action
- Conduct the meeting in a relaxed setting
- Have positive discussions and good give-and-take
- No blame and no gotchas
- Document the session
- Follow-up

In Closing

1. Throw out everything you know about challenging people. Insight prompts give you a painless way to do that and can easily be used with in-office and remote workers.
2. Use these prompts whenever you meet resistance to change: regardless of whether it is because you need to alter your strategy, adopt a new vision, or improve culture, craft an insight prompt to move people along.
3. Insight prompts have been around, but they have never been applied in a consistent and disciplined way. You can remedy that.
4. Remember, an insight prompt is a polite nudge to urge others to think, gain insight, and then change behavior. That is what good frontline managers want.

CHAPTER 10:
How to Easily Give and Receive Feedback

Annual feedback sessions are ineffective. As humans, we tend to take criticism of ourselves personally. A corporate executive board study shows that yearly feedback sessions significantly reduce employee performance.

Use the feedback brain tricks in this chapter to make a tough job more manageable.

Check-ins

Enlightened organizations have replaced annual feedback sessions with "check-ins," where managers informally ask questions such as:

- What was the highlight of your week?
- Is there anything you need help with?
- What are your priorities this week?

The more frequently check-ins are done, the easier they are to do because they become your habit. And the more often they are done, the more helpful they are to the recipient. No one likes operating in the dark.

Positive feedback

Don't forget to give positive feedback. It is easy to overlook this when you assume everyone knows they are doing a good job. They don't. Plus everyone likes praise. So, if you see a behavior that assists you in achieving results or helps in completing the mission, promptly praise it. When it comes to employee performance, psychologists say reward beats punishment every time.

Brain Trick 1: Always Use Future Tense

When giving or getting feedback, use the future tense. If you give feedback in the past tense, the recipient's brain senses it as blame. When feedback is in future tense, the brain interprets it as helpful. Here is an example:

Past tense: Matt, in yesterday's presentation on slide three, you said,
"ABC," which put off the client. You should have said, "XYZ."

Future tense: Matt, I was thinking about how we could make the presentation even better. In the future, we could say "XYZ" on that third slide because the client will love it.

In the past tense example, Matt goes away in anger, even though he doesn't show it. In the future tense example, Matt is pleased because he feels you helped him.

Brain Trick 2: Ask for Feedback

Neuroscientists recently found that giving and getting feedback is more comfortable and more effective if you ask for it. Some companies require employees (and bosses) to periodically ask for feedback. Consider requiring your direct reports to ask for feedback every week or two. It takes away some of the sting for both of you.

Brain Trick 3: Ask for Permission to Give or Get Feedback

If you walk up and blurt out negative feedback, it is like dousing someone with cold water. A lead-in takes away some of the sting:

- "May I offer some feedback?"
- "Would you like some feedback?"
- "Could I ask you for some feedback?"

Brain trick 4: Ask for Feedback on Getting Feedback

Elicit ideas from your employees on how you can get more feedback to help you perform better. After all, it's easier to ask them for ideas on how to get feedback—feedback mechanisms—than it is for them to give you feedback. Once you introduce the feedback channel they recommend, they will feel a sense of ownership and will feel more comfortable using it.

When you ask your employees or co-workers the question, "How would you feel most comfortable giving me pointers or comments?" you'll get solid gold feedback on ways to get feedback.

Quotes

"There is more to feedback than just listening to what your employees are saying. Every leader needs sources of information he can trust—someone who is an impartial observer and can whisper in your ear and provide reliable ground truth on what is happening in the organization.

The best leaders have an insatiable appetite for information, whether it's substantive or scuttlebutt. They are aware of everything going on in their domain."
— Skotty Skotzko, retired government executive

"The advice I would give would be to first figure out a way to get feedback that's honest and to give feedback that's honest. Wherever you've fallen down on the job, other people know about it and you probably don't. So, there's got to be a way of finding out how well you're doing for the purpose of doing better."
– Bob Herd, retired government executive

CHAPTER 11:
How to Listen Actively

The ability to effectively listen is an essential component of leadership, but few leaders know just what it takes to become a better listener. You can improve your ability to effectively lead by learning the skills for active listening.

Active listening involves paying attention, withholding judgment, reflecting, clarifying, summarizing, and sharing. Each listening skill requires several techniques or behaviors.

SIX SKILLS THAT CONTRIBUTE TO ACTIVE LISTENING

1. **Pay attention:** One goal of active listening is to set a relaxed tone and allow time and opportunity for the other person to think and speak. Pay attention to your frame of mind and your body language. Be focused on the moment and operate from a place of respect.

2. **Withhold judgment:** Active listening requires an open mind. As a listener and a leader, you need to be open to new ideas, perspectives, and possibilities. Even when good listeners have strong views, they suspend judgment, hold their criticism, and avoid arguing or selling points right away.

3. **Reflect:** Learn to mirror the other person's information and emotions by paraphrasing key points. Please don't assume that you understand correctly or that the other person knows you've heard him. Reflecting is a way to indicate that you and your counterpart are on the same page.

4. **Clarify:** Don't be shy to ask questions about any issue that is ambiguous or unclear. Open-ended, clarifying, and probing questions are essential tools. They draw people out and encourage them to expand their ideas while inviting reflection and thoughtful response.

5. **Summarize:** Restating critical themes as the conversation proceeds confirms and solidifies your grasp of the other person's point of view. It also helps both parties to be clear on mutual responsibilities and follow-up. Briefly summarize what you have understood as you listened, and ask the other person to do the same.

6. **Share:** Active listening is first about understanding the other person and then about being perceived. As you gain a clearer understanding of the other person's perspective, you can introduce your ideas, feelings, and suggestions. You might talk about a similar experience you had or share an idea triggered by a comment previously made in the conversation.

CHAPTER 12:
How to Ask Powerful Questions

Questions are a powerful tool for all managers, and they are little miracles because of what they do inside your brain. For instance, we all think we can multi-task, but our brain's internal focusing mechanism is merely switching focus back and forth. Your brain can only hold one idea at a time. So, when we hear a question, the brain unconditionally focuses on it.

If you need to get someone's attention, ask a question. A question forces mental processes to stop. Questions trigger consideration and thinking, whereas imperatives and statements don't. They are powerful, so, if the concept is complicated, don't put anyone on the spot—give them time to think and get back to you.

Why and *how* are the most compelling questions. But *what* questions can be powerful as well:

What's possible here? How can we. ..?

Here is another tip: ask positive questions. In the old days, we analyzed organizations using SWOT analysis, or Strengths, Weaknesses, Opportunities, and Threats. Notice two of these, weaknesses and threats, are negatives. Psychologists have found that discussing or thinking about negatives temporarily changes the brain and reduces the brain's ability to reach creative conclusions.

So, couch your questions positively. Instead of asking the negative, "What stops us from taking more risks?" use the positive, "What can we do to take more prudent risks?"

Or, instead of asking, "What assumptions hold us back?" ask, "What does it take to be successful in our organization?"

When you fill out your to-do list, add a few questions to it to ask each day. Think about whether you need to aim your questions at a group or an individual employee. See the chart on the next page for powerful questions you can use for discovery, problem-solving, action, and learning.

Earlier, in chapter two, we looked at four different principles that are typically present in great leaders. These principles include valuing others, giving to others, connecting with others, and involving others. In chapter two, we looked at a graphic that outlined different behaviors and outcomes that helped explain how and why these principles are significant. Below are some reinforcing questions that you can ask that will help develop these principles to better lead your employees:

Value Others:
- How are you doing?
- How are you really doing?
- What can I do this week to best help you?
- What concerns you the most over the short term? The long term?
- If you could design your perfect day, what would it look like?

Give (Law of Reciprocity):
- What additional information would you like?
- Do you prefer public or private recognition? (followed by a compliment)
- How do you feel most comfortable when participating with the team?
- Do you feel ready to experiment with a new task?

Connect (Deep Communication):
- How do you think your job links to the big picture?
- What do you see as our core issues?

- What are your priorities this week?
- How can the team communicate better?

Challenge Others (Include in Problem Solving):
- *Let me know Monday (To maximize effectiveness, give them time to think, but also give them a firm deadline):*
    - What can we change to be more efficient?
    - What three things can we do to collaborate with our sister organizations?
    - Can you help me brainstorm some new approaches?

ACTION LEARNING PHASE	QUESTION DRIVERS	EXAMPLES
FRAME	- Importance - Perspective - Intentions - Assumptions - Patterns - Dilemmas - Uncertainties - Opportunities - Outcomes - Experience - Knowledge gaps	- Why is this important? To you? To us? - What questions would our stakeholders ask? - What do we want to happen? - What assumptions are we making here? - What are the themes that are emerging? - What are the struggles you have faced? - What do we need to know? - Is there an opportunity in this challenge? - What does success look like? - What have others done here? - What haven't you told us that we might need to know?
SOLVE	- Connections - New possibilities - Creativity - New meaning - Stakeholders - First steps	- What would happen if we connected A and B? - What if we tried...? - What feels impossible? What would fail to solve it? - How would success affect our overall mission? - Who cares about the outcome? Solving this? - What is a first step we could take?
ACT	- Change - Resistance - Engagement - Energy - Support	- What will that action get us? - What barriers will we face in taking action? - Who will oppose this action? How can we involve them? - Who will support this action? How can we leverage them? - How will we keep ourselves motivated? - What support do we need?
LEARN	- Problem-solving - Peer group dynamics - Self-awareness	- What am I learning about problem-solving? In a group? - What did we learn about ourselves as leaders? - What did we learn about ourselves as problem-solvers? - How can we prevent this problem from reoccurring? - What did we learn about our organizational culture? - What can we take back and apply in our workplace?

Quote

"Great Leaders Ask Great Questions."
— Peter Drucker

CHAPTER 13:
Leadership Tip Sheet

Leadership Is… Inspiring others to change (higher performance/different direction)	
Motivators • Mission success • Relationships • Recognition • Team success • Challenging/important work • Overcoming a challenge • Leaving a legacy • Fair and frequent feedback	**Reciprocity (Gifts to instill trust and influence)** • Attention • Time • Recognition • Respect • Information • Resources • Power • Opportunity • Follow-through • Feedback • Clear expectations • Understanding • Empathy • Looking out for his/her people (wing-man) • Chance to fail ("get out of jail" free card) • Face-to-face interaction
Six Steps to Great Leadership 1. Establish safety (remove fear) 2. Establish trust (see reciprocity) 3. Establish clarity (see communications) 4. Establish challenges—insight prompts 5. Get feedback 6. Follow-up	
Three Leadership Blocks • If you tell them, they won't do it • What's in your head is not in theirs • They won't tell you what's in their heads	**Communications Approaches** • One way: order giving, transmitting • Two way: intentional conversations, casual conversations, empathetic conversations Great leaders use more two-way, less one-way approaches
Management Levers • Organizational design • Staffing • Measurement • Training • Rewards • Communications	**Leadership Behaviors** • Acknowledge (smile) and show empathy/concern • Connect (see two-way communications approaches) • Give (See reciprocity—builds trust) • Invite participation (ideas, decisions, plans) THEN • Nudge—give thought homework and follow-up
Best Boss • Passionate • Has good knowledge of and is comfortable in the work environment • Demonstrates integrity • Communicates well • Believes in work–life balance • Delegates/gets consensus • Respects the opinions of others • Cares for his/her people • Solicits opinions from the staff • Listens well • Values failure	**Worst Boss** • Controlling • Screams/yells at people • Not accessible • Vindictive • Risk adverse • Is a sycophant • Appears apathetic • Does not provide feedback
	The Golden Offer: Don't keep us in the dark, let us know what you want and why, be positive, give us leeway to be creative, and tell us how we are doing; then we'll outperform for you

CHAPTER 14: Recommended Reading

Leadership and Self-Deception, The Arbinger Institute, 2000

Crucial Conversations, Kerry Patterson, 2011

Thinking Fast and Slow, Daniel Kahneman, 2013

Leadership Elements, A Guide to Building Trust, Mike Mears, 2013

Atomic Habits, James Clear, 2018

The Power of Habit, Charles Duhigg, 2012

Human Side of Enterprise, Douglas MacGregor, 1960

Influence without Authority, Allan R. Cohen and David L. Bradford, 1989

Bureaucracy, James Q. Wilson, 1989

Driven, Paul R. Lawrence and Nitin Nohria, 2002

The Character of a Leader, Donald Alexander, 2013

Background A

- Final Reminders
- Detailed Brain Model

- Government Executive Interview

Final Reminders:

- NNSA has a vital mission and has entrusted you to lead their employees; so, review this book frequently to sharpen your skills.

- Leaders must be seen to be heard. Get away from your desk as much as you can, even if it involves renegotiating with your boss to shift or delegate some current responsibilities.

- It is okay to share genuine emotions and speak from the heart. Making a mistake here or there and admitting it, or being a little vulnerable at times, shows authenticity and can help build trust.

- Repetition and your own longevity greatly boost the chance for the success of your message.

- You can change employee behaviors. Carefully orchestrated insight prompts can help change behaviors without humiliating people. If you change employee behaviors for a sufficiently long time, culture changes.

- Create an environment wherein direct reports can have a little fun and urge them to do the same with their peers. Innovation and big ideas often erupt from fun.

Detailed Brain Model

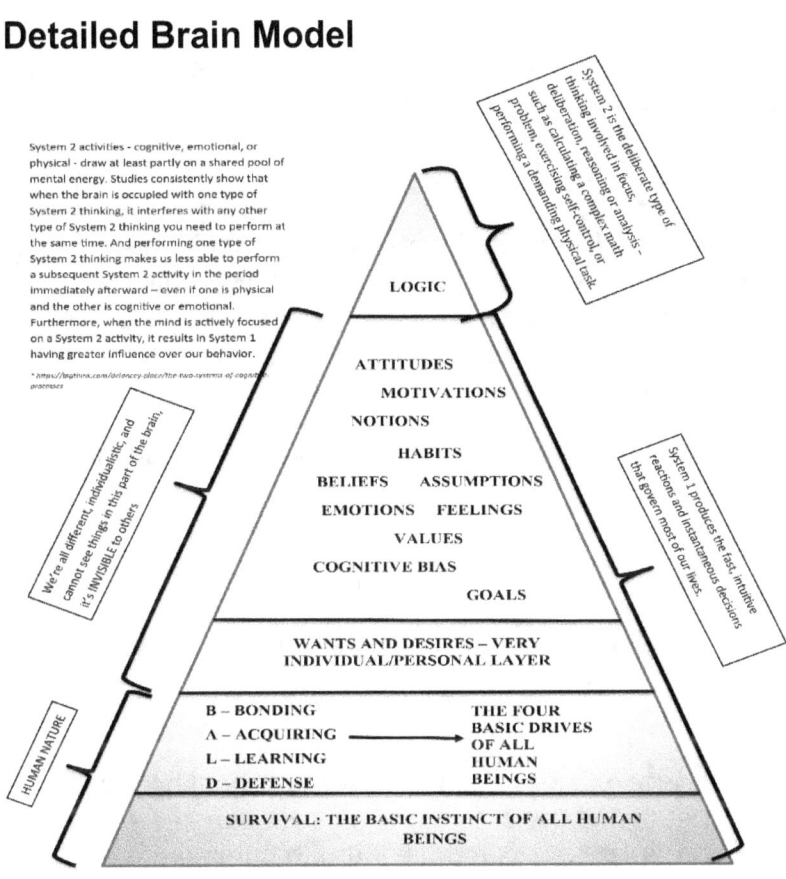

We operate in the System I - intuitive, automatic brain - roughly 85% of time with habits, impulse decisions, unconscious routines, etc. We spend approximately 15% on reasoning and thinking, which uses most of our brain energy.

Government executive interview (with Leo Hazlewood)

Numerous government and private sector employees called Leo A. Hazlewood "the best leader I ever knew." Currently a Senior Vice President at Science Applications International Corporation, Mr. Hazlewood served as the first Deputy Director of NGA. His assignments at CIA included: Comptroller; Director, National Photographic Interpretation Center; and Executive Director for Administration. Mr. Hazlewood received his A.B. from Georgetown University, an A.M. from the University of Illinois (Urbana), and a Ph.D. from the University of Pennsylvania.

I talked with Leo about his management and leadership style and lessons learned.

MM:

What advice would you give a new executive?

LH:

Every executive is frustrated over how hard it is to get things done across the strata of an organization. You must learn to communicate and link the importance of the mission to people so they will work together the mission. You have to work through people across the organization in order to solve problems and move the organization forward.

An executive must have a direction toward which he or she wants to move the organization. They should begin with a small set of critical issues. Address each issue with a plan and communicate consistently your vision and plans. It is impossible to spend too much time repeating your direction or vision. You should repeat your direction and expectations until you can no longer stand it.

Next, you must tie rewards and resource allocation toward realizing the plans. Cascade the direction down the chain through individual's performance objectives. Reward progress.

I guess the final piece of advice to this new executive is to share knowledge. Counsel and mentor the next generation of leaders and managers; those who will be moving into the executive realm in the next three to five years. Part of your job is to build the next generation. This will take a great deal of your time and personal involvement. Good senior leaders must teach the junior leaders through conversation, listening, and storytelling.

MM:

How do you get employees onboard with your goals and vision?

LH:

I believe people deep down are motivated by their connection to the mission. Every organization has a caste system and a leader must show every caste how they are important to the organization's mission.

MM:

Do you meet with each employee individually?

LH:

No. That is not practical, nor is it especially useful. But I do

make it a point to be seen outside my office with employees where they work. One day per month I go out and work with the troops. I visited with office workers, dock workers. Sometimes when I work late, I go out and visit with employees on the second or third shift. I tell what I am thinking about and I asked for their feedback and perception of what's happening.

You absolutely have to find the time to have more face-to-face contact. George Bush Senior, when he was at the Agency, understood that. George was one of the rare Directors of Central intelligence who walked through the front door in the morning rather than through the garage ... so did John Deutch. The difference was that Bush said hello to everyone he met and talked to people. Everyone remembers that.

You do not have to talk to everyone. But the fact that you are seen and talk with many different people, in different castes, is noticed. Those you talk with will help spread your vision and your values. I found that telling stories was a great way to share my vision and values. Good stories get retold and help spread the message. They become part of the oral history of the organization.

When you get up close and personal with employees, you give people clarity of purpose. It is also essential that you are candid with the employees. Give positive feedback when it is deserved and be candid when you see the need for improvement. And remember to live the values you espouse. Employees are very sensitive to the way they see you behave. If there is a conflict between what you say and what you do, they will believe what you do.

MM:

What are the characteristics of a good story – one that will influence the organization?

LH:

If you are going through change, you need to communicate it and storytelling can be a great way to do that. It's a good way to build a committed leadership team and to share and spread best practices. Jim Taylor used to bring a monthly group together to talk about major issues, insights into challenges, and how they thought about problems. Often, the greatest and most powerful stories told in those sessions were about "the worst time of our lives." Stories communicate with people in an intuitive way – much better than lectures. Stories must be real.

MM:

You value informal, personal contact with employees across the organization. What about more formal meetings?

LH:

I used to have town hall meetings every two months for Q&A about our direction and vision. This is tough to do because it takes so much time. But you have to have ruthless discipline to stay with what you have scheduled.

Formal training sessions are another great way to impact organizational thinking and to get feedback. Do the Jack Welch thing at training sessions and don't lecture. Talk for 10 or 15 minutes about your direction and maybe a pressing issue and then ask questions. Listen. Start a dialogue because that's how you can get your purpose across. *Listen!*

I spent one entire week with executives at their new training course and learned an incredible amount I never would have otherwise. In those training sessions, your hear things you would never hear and you get asked questions they would never ask during routine day-to-day business activities.

Another effective formal meeting tactic is to have small off-site meetings between a senior executive and groups of staff. Ray Hufstettler (ed. Senior agency executive) would pull together a cross section of employees and go off-site for a day. The employees would be broken up into small groups. The group would discuss a challenge – say barriers to success – and then report out at the end of the day. Ray would then meet with the entire group to address the issues raised and build an action plan to implement necessary changes. This took two days out his schedule, but it built buy-in and cohesion. This worked because of Ray's personal involvement. [See NPIC Case Study in next tab.]

If you can't do an off-site, you can form a panel of executives to answer questions from managers and employees during a short Q&A. This shares information and lets the staff see the operating values first hand. This all takes time and personal involvement but you have to be touched by the rank and file. You have to get out of your office.

You can also schedule a meeting to talk about successes and celebrate turnarounds. Let your junior managers talk about what they did and how they did it. This helps spread desired behaviors.

MM:

What other techniques have you found useful to stay in touch and affect change?

LH:

I used to poll staff opinion and experience on some basic questions that affect organizational health and management strength. Simple yes/no or multiple choice for about 10 questions. Then I would total the results and post them. Let the workforce see that you are interested in and using the information. It will help build trust and they will be more forthcoming in the future. If cultural or personnel problems show up frequently, deal with them openly. Trust your employee's feedback on people problems and organizational challenges.

MM:
Is there anything you would like to say in closing?

LH:

Your time is your most valuable asset. Allow yourself time to reflect and show your priorities by voting with your calendar. Stay in touch with the people below you. Give your employees challenging work and make sure that they have first-line supervisors they trust. Invest in training and education and make sure that all employees have a path for professional growth.

About the Author

Mike Mears is a leadership speaker and consultant to government and private sector organizations. Along with his CIA operational experience, Mike founded and headed the CIA Leadership Academy. He retired as the Agency's Chief of Human Capital in 2006.

Prior to joining the CIA, Mike was senior vice president at GE investments where he managed private equity funds, was a turnaround specialist, and a Six Sigma Black Belt. Before that, he launched eleven small business start-ups, and was president of a fast-food company. Mike served as commander of a nuclear missile site, a general's aide, and as a combat platoon leader in Vietnam where he was decorated for valor.

Mike earned his undergraduate degree at the U.S. Military Academy at West Point and his MBA from Harvard Business School.

In addition to consulting, Mike teaches or lectures on leadership at the Department of Defense, National Intelligence University, Georgetown, the University of Salzburg, and the University of Maryland.

Mike's upcoming book is Mindbending! How Great Bosses Plant Mental Seeds to Energize Employees and Change Culture.

www.ingramcontent.com/pod-product-compliance
Lightning Source LLC
Chambersburg PA
CBHW070455220526
45466CB00004B/1839